Remember to Give *Thanks!*

Gratitude Planner and Journal.

Activinotes

Activinotes

DAILY JOURNALS, PLANNERS, NOTEBOOKS AND OTHER BLANK BOOKS

All Rights reserved. No part of this book may be reproduced or used in any way or form or by any means whether electronic or mechanical, this means that you cannot record or photocopy any material ideas or tips that are provided in this book.

Copyright 2016

Gratitude Planner and Journal

Things to be thankful for

date
_____

to do list:

The best part of my day

Notes

Gratitude Planner and Journal

Things to be thankful for

date
_____

to do list:

The best part of my day

Notes

Gratitude Planner and Journal

Things to be thankful for

_____
_____
_____
_____
_____
_____
_____
_____

date
_____

to do list:

_____ ☐
_____ ☐
_____ ☐
_____ ☐
_____ ☐
_____ ☐
_____ ☐
_____ ☐
_____ ☐

The best part of my day

_____
_____
_____
_____
_____
_____
_____
_____

Notes

Gratitude Planner and Journal

Things to be thankful for

date
_____

to do list:

The best part of my day

Notes

Gratitude Planner and Journal

Things to be thankful for

_____
_____
_____
_____
_____
_____
_____
_____
_____

date
_____

to do list:

_____ ☐
_____ ☐
_____ ☐
_____ ☐
_____ ☐
_____ ☐
_____ ☐
_____ ☐
_____ ☐

The best part of my day

_____
_____
_____
_____
_____
_____
_____
_____
_____
_____
_____

Notes

Gratitude Planner and Journal

Things to be thankful for

date
_____

to do list:

The best part of my day

Notes

Gratitude Planner and Journal

Things to be thankful for

_____
_____
_____
_____
_____
_____
_____
_____

date
_____

to do list:

_____ ☐
_____ ☐
_____ ☐
_____ ☐
_____ ☐
_____ ☐
_____ ☐
_____ ☐
_____ ☐

The best part of my day

_____
_____
_____
_____
_____
_____
_____
_____

Notes

Gratitude Planner and Journal

Things to be thankful for

_____
_____
_____
_____
_____
_____
_____
_____
_____

date
_____

to do list:

_____ ☐
_____ ☐
_____ ☐
_____ ☐
_____ ☐
_____ ☐
_____ ☐
_____ ☐
_____ ☐

The best part of my day

_____
_____
_____
_____
_____
_____
_____
_____

Notes

Gratitude Planner and Journal

Things to be thankful for

_____
_____
_____
_____
_____
_____
_____
_____
_____
_____

date
_____

to do list:

_____ ☐
_____ ☐
_____ ☐
_____ ☐
_____ ☐
_____ ☐
_____ ☐
_____ ☐
_____ ☐

The best part of my day

_____
_____
_____
_____
_____
_____
_____
_____
_____
_____

Notes

Gratitude Planner and Journal

Things to be thankful for

_____
_____
_____
_____
_____
_____
_____
_____
_____

date
_____

to do list:

_____ ☐
_____ ☐
_____ ☐
_____ ☐
_____ ☐
_____ ☐
_____ ☐
_____ ☐
_____ ☐

The best part of my day

_____
_____
_____
_____
_____
_____
_____
_____

Notes

Gratitude Planner and Journal

Things to be thankful for

_____
_____
_____
_____
_____
_____
_____
_____
_____

date
_____

to do list:

_____ ☐
_____ ☐
_____ ☐
_____ ☐
_____ ☐
_____ ☐
_____ ☐
_____ ☐
_____ ☐

The best part of my day

_____
_____
_____
_____
_____
_____
_____
_____
_____

Notes

_____
_____
_____
_____
_____
_____
_____
_____

Gratitude Planner and Journal

Things to be thankful for

_____

_____

_____

_____

_____

_____

_____

_____

date
_____

to do list:

_____ ☐

_____ ☐

_____ ☐

_____ ☐

_____ ☐

_____ ☐

_____ ☐

_____ ☐

_____ ☐

The best part of my day

_____

_____

_____

_____

_____

_____

_____

_____

_____

_____

_____

Notes

Gratitude Planner and Journal

Things to be thankful for

_____
_____
_____
_____
_____
_____
_____
_____

date

_____

to do list:

_____ ☐
_____ ☐
_____ ☐
_____ ☐
_____ ☐
_____ ☐
_____ ☐
_____ ☐
_____ ☐

The best part of my day

_____
_____
_____
_____
_____
_____
_____
_____
_____

Notes

Gratitude Planner and Journal

Things to be thankful for

_____
_____
_____
_____
_____
_____
_____
_____

date
_____

to do list:

_____ ☐
_____ ☐
_____ ☐
_____ ☐
_____ ☐
_____ ☐
_____ ☐
_____ ☐
_____ ☐

The best part of my day

_____
_____
_____
_____
_____
_____
_____
_____

Notes

Gratitude Planner and Journal

Things to be thankful for

date
_____

to do list:

The best part of my day

Notes

Gratitude Planner and Journal

Things to be thankful for

date
_____

to do list:

The best part of my day

Notes

Gratitude Planner and Journal

Things to be thankful for

_____
_____
_____
_____
_____
_____
_____
_____
_____

date
_____

to do list:

_____ ☐
_____ ☐
_____ ☐
_____ ☐
_____ ☐
_____ ☐
_____ ☐
_____ ☐
_____ ☐

The best part of my day

_____
_____
_____
_____
_____
_____
_____
_____
_____
_____
_____

Notes

_____
_____
_____
_____
_____
_____
_____
_____
_____
_____

Gratitude Planner and Journal

Things to be thankful for

date
_____

to do list:

The best part of my day

Notes

Gratitude Planner and Journal

Things to be thankful for

_____

date
_____

to do list:

□
□
□
□
□
□
□
□
□

The best part of my day

Notes

Gratitude Planner and Journal

Things to be thankful for

_____
_____
_____
_____
_____
_____
_____
_____

date
_____

to do list:

_____ ☐
_____ ☐
_____ ☐
_____ ☐
_____ ☐
_____ ☐
_____ ☐
_____ ☐
_____ ☐

The best part of my day

_____
_____
_____
_____
_____
_____
_____
_____

Notes

Gratitude Planner and Journal

Things to be thankful for

_____
_____
_____
_____
_____
_____
_____
_____
_____
_____

date
_____

to do list:

_____ ☐
_____ ☐
_____ ☐
_____ ☐
_____ ☐
_____ ☐
_____ ☐
_____ ☐
_____ ☐

The best part of my day

_____
_____
_____
_____
_____
_____
_____
_____
_____
_____

Notes

Gratitude Planner and Journal

Things to be thankful for

_____
_____
_____
_____
_____
_____
_____
_____
_____

date
_____

to do list:

_____ ☐
_____ ☐
_____ ☐
_____ ☐
_____ ☐
_____ ☐
_____ ☐
_____ ☐
_____ ☐

The best part of my day

_____
_____
_____
_____
_____
_____
_____
_____

Notes

Gratitude Planner and Journal

Things to be thankful for

date

_____

to do list:

The best part of my day

Notes

Gratitude Planner and Journal

Things to be thankful for

_____
_____
_____
_____
_____
_____
_____
_____

date
_____

to do list:

_____ ☐
_____ ☐
_____ ☐
_____ ☐
_____ ☐
_____ ☐
_____ ☐
_____ ☐
_____ ☐

The best part of my day

_____
_____
_____
_____
_____
_____
_____
_____

Notes

Gratitude Planner and Journal

Things to be thankful for

_____
_____
_____
_____
_____
_____
_____
_____
_____

date
_____

to do list:

_____ ☐
_____ ☐
_____ ☐
_____ ☐
_____ ☐
_____ ☐
_____ ☐
_____ ☐
_____ ☐

The best part of my day

_____
_____
_____
_____
_____
_____
_____
_____
_____
_____

Notes

_____
_____
_____
_____
_____
_____
_____
_____
_____
_____
_____

Gratitude Planner and Journal

Things to be thankful for

_____
_____
_____
_____
_____
_____
_____
_____

date
_____

to do list:

_____ ☐
_____ ☐
_____ ☐
_____ ☐
_____ ☐
_____ ☐
_____ ☐
_____ ☐
_____ ☐

The best part of my day

_____
_____
_____
_____
_____
_____
_____
_____
_____

Notes

Gratitude Planner and Journal

Things to be thankful for

_____
_____
_____
_____
_____
_____
_____
_____

date
_____

to do list:

_____ ☐
_____ ☐
_____ ☐
_____ ☐
_____ ☐
_____ ☐
_____ ☐
_____ ☐

The best part of my day

_____
_____
_____
_____
_____
_____
_____
_____

Notes

Gratitude Planner and Journal

Things to be thankful for

_____
_____
_____
_____
_____
_____
_____
_____
_____

date
_____

to do list:

_____ ☐
_____ ☐
_____ ☐
_____ ☐
_____ ☐
_____ ☐
_____ ☐
_____ ☐
_____ ☐

The best part of my day

_____
_____
_____
_____
_____
_____
_____
_____
_____
_____

Notes

Gratitude Planner and Journal

Things to be thankful for

_____
_____
_____
_____
_____
_____
_____
_____
_____

date
_____

to do list:

_____ ☐
_____ ☐
_____ ☐
_____ ☐
_____ ☐
_____ ☐
_____ ☐
_____ ☐
_____ ☐

The best part of my day

_____
_____
_____
_____
_____
_____
_____
_____
_____
_____
_____

Notes

Gratitude Planner and Journal

Things to be thankful for

date
_____

to do list:

The best part of my day

Notes

Gratitude Planner and Journal

Things to be thankful for

_____
_____
_____
_____
_____
_____
_____
_____

date
_____

to do list:

_____ ☐
_____ ☐
_____ ☐
_____ ☐
_____ ☐
_____ ☐
_____ ☐
_____ ☐
_____ ☐

The best part of my day

_____
_____
_____
_____
_____
_____
_____
_____

Notes

Gratitude Planner and Journal

Things to be thankful for

_____
_____
_____
_____
_____
_____
_____
_____
_____

date
_____

to do list:

_____ ☐
_____ ☐
_____ ☐
_____ ☐
_____ ☐
_____ ☐
_____ ☐
_____ ☐
_____ ☐

The best part of my day

_____
_____
_____
_____
_____
_____
_____
_____
_____
_____

Notes

Gratitude Planner and Journal

Things to be thankful for

date
_____

to do list:

☐
☐
☐
☐
☐
☐
☐
☐
☐

The best part of my day

Notes

Gratitude Planner and Journal

Things to be thankful for

date
_____

to do list:

The best part of my day

Notes

Gratitude Planner and Journal

Things to be thankful for

_____
_____
_____
_____
_____
_____
_____
_____
_____

date
_____

to do list:

_____ ☐
_____ ☐
_____ ☐
_____ ☐
_____ ☐
_____ ☐
_____ ☐
_____ ☐
_____ ☐

The best part of my day

_____
_____
_____
_____
_____
_____
_____
_____
_____
_____

Notes

Gratitude Planner and Journal

Things to be
thankful for

date
_____

to do list:

The best part
of my day

Notes

Gratitude Planner and Journal

Things to be thankful for

_____
_____
_____
_____
_____
_____
_____
_____

date
_____

to do list:

_____ ☐
_____ ☐
_____ ☐
_____ ☐
_____ ☐
_____ ☐
_____ ☐
_____ ☐
_____ ☐

The best part of my day

_____
_____
_____
_____
_____
_____
_____
_____
_____
_____

Notes

Gratitude Planner and Journal

Things to be thankful for

date
_____

to do list:

☐
☐
☐
☐
☐
☐
☐
☐
☐

The best part of my day

Notes

Gratitude Planner and Journal

Things to be thankful for

date
_____

to do list:

The best part of my day

Notes

Gratitude Planner and Journal

Things to be thankful for

date
_____

to do list:

The best part of my day

Notes

Gratitude Planner and Journal

Things to be thankful for

date
_____

to do list:

The best part of my day

Notes

Gratitude Planner and Journal

Things to be
thankful for

date
_____

to do list:

The best part
of my day

Notes

Gratitude Planner and Journal

Things to be thankful for

_____
_____
_____
_____
_____
_____
_____
_____
_____
_____

date

_____

to do list:

_____ ☐
_____ ☐
_____ ☐
_____ ☐
_____ ☐
_____ ☐
_____ ☐
_____ ☐
_____ ☐

The best part of my day

_____
_____
_____
_____
_____
_____
_____
_____
_____
_____
_____

Notes

_____
_____
_____
_____
_____
_____
_____
_____
_____

Gratitude Planner and Journal

Things to be thankful for

_____
_____
_____
_____
_____
_____
_____
_____
_____

date
_____

to do list:

_____ ☐
_____ ☐
_____ ☐
_____ ☐
_____ ☐
_____ ☐
_____ ☐
_____ ☐
_____ ☐

The best part of my day

_____
_____
_____
_____
_____
_____
_____
_____
_____

Notes

Gratitude Planner and Journal

Things to be thankful for

date
_____

to do list:

The best part of my day

Notes

Gratitude Planner and Journal

Things to be thankful for

_____
_____
_____
_____
_____
_____
_____
_____
_____
_____

date
_____

to do list:

_____ ☐
_____ ☐
_____ ☐
_____ ☐
_____ ☐
_____ ☐
_____ ☐
_____ ☐
_____ ☐

The best part of my day

_____
_____
_____
_____
_____
_____
_____
_____
_____

Notes

Gratitude Planner and Journal

Things to be thankful for

date

_____

to do list:

The best part of my day

Notes

Gratitude Planner and Journal

Things to be thankful for

_____

_____

_____

_____

_____

_____

_____

_____

date

_____

to do list:

_____ ☐

_____ ☐

_____ ☐

_____ ☐

_____ ☐

_____ ☐

_____ ☐

_____ ☐

_____ ☐

The best part of my day

_____

_____

_____

_____

_____

_____

_____

_____

Notes

Gratitude Planner and Journal

Things to be thankful for

date
_____

to do list:

The best part of my day

Notes

Gratitude Planner and Journal

Things to be thankful for

date
_____

to do list:

☐
☐
☐
☐
☐
☐
☐
☐
☐

The best part of my day

Notes

Gratitude Planner and Journal

Things to be thankful for

date
_____

to do list:

The best part of my day

Notes

Gratitude Planner and Journal

Things to be thankful for

date
_____

to do list:

The best part of my day

Notes

Gratitude Planner and Journal

Things to be thankful for

_____
_____
_____
_____
_____
_____
_____
_____
_____

date
_____

to do list:

_____ ☐
_____ ☐
_____ ☐
_____ ☐
_____ ☐
_____ ☐
_____ ☐
_____ ☐
_____ ☐

The best part of my day

_____
_____
_____
_____
_____
_____
_____
_____
_____

Notes

_____
_____
_____
_____
_____
_____
_____

Gratitude Planner and Journal

Things to be thankful for

_____

_____

_____

_____

_____

_____

_____

_____

_____

date

_____

to do list:

_____ ☐

_____ ☐

_____ ☐

_____ ☐

_____ ☐

_____ ☐

_____ ☐

_____ ☐

_____ ☐

The best part of my day

_____

_____

_____

_____

_____

_____

_____

_____

_____

Notes

Gratitude Planner and Journal

Things to be thankful for

_____
_____
_____
_____
_____
_____
_____
_____
_____

date
_____

to do list:

_____ ☐
_____ ☐
_____ ☐
_____ ☐
_____ ☐
_____ ☐
_____ ☐
_____ ☐
_____ ☐

The best part of my day

_____
_____
_____
_____
_____
_____
_____
_____
_____
_____

Notes

_____
_____
_____
_____
_____
_____
_____
_____
_____
_____
_____

Gratitude Planner and Journal

Things to be thankful for

date
_____

to do list:

The best part of my day

Notes

Gratitude Planner and Journal

Things to be thankful for

_____
_____
_____
_____
_____
_____
_____
_____
_____

date

_____

to do list:

_____ ☐
_____ ☐
_____ ☐
_____ ☐
_____ ☐
_____ ☐
_____ ☐
_____ ☐
_____ ☐

The best part of my day

_____
_____
_____
_____
_____
_____
_____
_____
_____
_____
_____

Notes

Gratitude Planner and Journal

Things to be thankful for

_____
_____
_____
_____
_____
_____
_____
_____
_____

date
_____

to do list:

_____ ☐
_____ ☐
_____ ☐
_____ ☐
_____ ☐
_____ ☐
_____ ☐
_____ ☐
_____ ☐

The best part of my day

_____
_____
_____
_____
_____
_____
_____
_____
_____

Notes

_____
_____
_____
_____
_____
_____
_____
_____

Gratitude Planner and Journal

Things to be
thankful for

date
_____

to do list:

The best part
of my day

Notes

Gratitude Planner and Journal

Things to be thankful for

_____
_____
_____
_____
_____
_____
_____
_____
_____

date
_____

to do list:

_____ ☐
_____ ☐
_____ ☐
_____ ☐
_____ ☐
_____ ☐
_____ ☐
_____ ☐
_____ ☐

The best part of my day

_____
_____
_____
_____
_____
_____
_____
_____
_____

Notes

Gratitude Planner and Journal

Things to be thankful for

date
_____

to do list:

☐
☐
☐
☐
☐
☐
☐
☐
☐

The best part of my day

Notes

Gratitude Planner and Journal

Things to be thankful for

date
_____

to do list:

☐
☐
☐
☐
☐
☐
☐
☐
☐

The best part of my day

Notes

Gratitude Planner and Journal

Things to be thankful for

_____
_____
_____
_____
_____
_____
_____
_____
_____

date
_____

to do list:

_____ ☐
_____ ☐
_____ ☐
_____ ☐
_____ ☐
_____ ☐
_____ ☐
_____ ☐
_____ ☐

The best part of my day

_____
_____
_____
_____
_____
_____
_____
_____
_____
_____
_____

Notes

Gratitude Planner and Journal

Things to be
thankful for

date
_____

to do list:

The best part
of my day

Notes

Gratitude Planner and Journal

Things to be thankful for

date
_____

to do list:

The best part of my day

Notes

Gratitude Planner and Journal

Things to be thankful for

date
_____

to do list:

The best part of my day

Notes

Gratitude Planner and Journal

Things to be thankful for

date
_____

to do list:

The best part of my day

Notes

Gratitude Planner and Journal

Things to be thankful for

_____

_____

_____

_____

_____

_____

_____

_____

_____

date
_____

to do list:

_____ ☐

_____ ☐

_____ ☐

_____ ☐

_____ ☐

_____ ☐

_____ ☐

_____ ☐

_____ ☐

The best part of my day

_____

_____

_____

_____

_____

_____

_____

_____

_____

Notes

_____

_____

_____

_____

_____

_____

_____

_____

_____

Gratitude Planner and Journal

Things to be thankful for

date
_____

to do list:

The best part of my day

Notes

Gratitude Planner and Journal

Things to be thankful for

_____
_____
_____
_____
_____
_____
_____
_____

date
_____

to do list:

_____ ☐
_____ ☐
_____ ☐
_____ ☐
_____ ☐
_____ ☐
_____ ☐
_____ ☐
_____ ☐

The best part of my day

_____
_____
_____
_____
_____
_____
_____
_____
_____
_____

Notes

_____
_____
_____
_____
_____
_____
_____
_____
_____

Gratitude Planner and Journal

Things to be thankful for

date
_____

to do list:

☐
☐
☐
☐
☐
☐
☐
☐
☐

The best part of my day

Notes

Gratitude Planner and Journal

Things to be thankful for

date
_____

to do list:

The best part of my day

Notes

Gratitude Planner and Journal

Things to be thankful for

date
_____

to do list:

☐
☐
☐
☐
☐
☐
☐
☐
☐

The best part of my day

Notes

Gratitude Planner and Journal

Things to be
thankful for

date
_____

to do list:

The best part
of my day

Notes

Gratitude Planner and Journal

Things to be thankful for

_____
_____
_____
_____
_____
_____
_____
_____
_____

date
_____

to do list:

- ☐ _____
- ☐ _____
- ☐ _____
- ☐ _____
- ☐ _____
- ☐ _____
- ☐ _____
- ☐ _____
- ☐ _____

The best part of my day

_____
_____
_____
_____
_____
_____
_____
_____
_____
_____

Notes

Gratitude Planner and Journal

Things to be
thankful for

date
_____

to do list:

The best part
of my day

Notes

Gratitude Planner and Journal

Things to be thankful for

date
_____

to do list:

The best part of my day

Notes

Gratitude Planner and Journal

Things to be thankful for

_____

_____

_____

_____

_____

_____

_____

_____

date
_____

to do list:

_____ ☐

_____ ☐

_____ ☐

_____ ☐

_____ ☐

_____ ☐

_____ ☐

_____ ☐

_____ ☐

The best part of my day

_____

_____

_____

_____

_____

_____

_____

_____

Notes

Gratitude Planner and Journal

Things to be thankful for

_____
_____
_____
_____
_____
_____
_____
_____

date

_____

to do list:

_____ ☐
_____ ☐
_____ ☐
_____ ☐
_____ ☐
_____ ☐
_____ ☐
_____ ☐
_____ ☐

The best part of my day

_____
_____
_____
_____
_____
_____
_____
_____
_____
_____

Notes

Gratitude Planner and Journal

Things to be thankful for

_____
_____
_____
_____
_____
_____
_____
_____
_____

date
_____

to do list:

_____ ☐
_____ ☐
_____ ☐
_____ ☐
_____ ☐
_____ ☐
_____ ☐
_____ ☐
_____ ☐

The best part of my day

_____
_____
_____
_____
_____
_____
_____
_____
_____

Notes

_____
_____
_____
_____
_____
_____
_____
_____
_____
_____

Gratitude Planner and Journal

Things to be thankful for

_____
_____
_____
_____
_____
_____
_____
_____

date
_____

to do list:

_____ ☐
_____ ☐
_____ ☐
_____ ☐
_____ ☐
_____ ☐
_____ ☐
_____ ☐
_____ ☐

The best part of my day

_____
_____
_____
_____
_____
_____
_____
_____
_____

Notes

Gratitude Planner and Journal

Things to be thankful for

_____
_____
_____
_____
_____
_____
_____
_____
_____
_____

date
_____

to do list:

_____ ☐
_____ ☐
_____ ☐
_____ ☐
_____ ☐
_____ ☐
_____ ☐
_____ ☐
_____ ☐

The best part of my day

_____
_____
_____
_____
_____
_____
_____
_____
_____
_____

Notes

Gratitude Planner and Journal

Things to be thankful for

_____
_____
_____
_____
_____
_____
_____
_____
_____

date
_____

to do list:

_____ ☐
_____ ☐
_____ ☐
_____ ☐
_____ ☐
_____ ☐
_____ ☐
_____ ☐
_____ ☐

The best part of my day

_____
_____
_____
_____
_____
_____
_____
_____
_____
_____

Notes

_____
_____
_____
_____
_____
_____
_____
_____

Gratitude Planner and Journal

Things to be thankful for

date
_____

to do list:

The best part of my day

Notes

Gratitude Planner and Journal

Things to be thankful for

_____

date
_____

to do list:

☐
☐
☐
☐
☐
☐
☐
☐
☐

The best part of my day

Notes

Gratitude Planner and Journal

Things to be thankful for

date
_____

to do list:

The best part of my day

Notes

Gratitude Planner and Journal

Things to be thankful for

_____
_____
_____
_____
_____
_____
_____
_____
_____
_____

date
_____

to do list:

_____ ☐
_____ ☐
_____ ☐
_____ ☐
_____ ☐
_____ ☐
_____ ☐
_____ ☐
_____ ☐

The best part of my day

_____
_____
_____
_____
_____
_____
_____
_____
_____
_____
_____

Notes

Gratitude Planner and Journal

Things to be thankful for

_____
_____
_____
_____
_____
_____
_____
_____
_____

date
_____

to do list:

_____ ☐
_____ ☐
_____ ☐
_____ ☐
_____ ☐
_____ ☐
_____ ☐
_____ ☐
_____ ☐

The best part of my day

_____
_____
_____
_____
_____
_____
_____
_____

Notes

_____
_____
_____
_____
_____
_____
_____
_____
_____

Gratitude Planner and Journal

Things to be thankful for

_____
_____
_____
_____
_____
_____
_____
_____
_____

date
_____

to do list:

_____ ☐
_____ ☐
_____ ☐
_____ ☐
_____ ☐
_____ ☐
_____ ☐
_____ ☐
_____ ☐

The best part of my day

_____
_____
_____
_____
_____
_____
_____
_____
_____

Notes

Gratitude Planner and Journal

Things to be thankful for

_____
_____
_____
_____
_____
_____
_____
_____

date
_____

to do list:

_____ ☐
_____ ☐
_____ ☐
_____ ☐
_____ ☐
_____ ☐
_____ ☐
_____ ☐
_____ ☐

The best part of my day

_____
_____
_____
_____
_____
_____
_____
_____

Notes

Gratitude Planner and Journal

Things to be thankful for

_____
_____
_____
_____
_____
_____
_____
_____
_____

date
_____

to do list:

_____ ☐
_____ ☐
_____ ☐
_____ ☐
_____ ☐
_____ ☐
_____ ☐
_____ ☐
_____ ☐

The best part of my day

_____
_____
_____
_____
_____
_____
_____
_____
_____

Notes

Gratitude Planner and Journal

Things to be thankful for

_____
_____
_____
_____
_____
_____
_____
_____
_____

date
_____

to do list:

_____ ☐
_____ ☐
_____ ☐
_____ ☐
_____ ☐
_____ ☐
_____ ☐
_____ ☐
_____ ☐

The best part of my day

_____
_____
_____
_____
_____
_____
_____
_____
_____

Notes

Gratitude Planner and Journal

Things to be thankful for

date
_____

to do list:

The best part of my day

Notes

Gratitude Planner and Journal

Things to be
thankful for

date
_____

to do list:

The best part
of my day

Notes

Gratitude Planner and Journal

Things to be thankful for

_____
_____
_____
_____
_____
_____
_____
_____
_____

date

_____

to do list:

_____ ☐
_____ ☐
_____ ☐
_____ ☐
_____ ☐
_____ ☐
_____ ☐
_____ ☐
_____ ☐

The best part of my day

_____
_____
_____
_____
_____
_____
_____
_____
_____

Notes

_____
_____
_____
_____
_____
_____
_____
_____
_____

Gratitude Planner and Journal

Things to be thankful for

date
_____

to do list:

The best part of my day

Notes

Gratitude Planner and Journal

Things to be thankful for

_____
_____
_____
_____
_____
_____
_____
_____
_____

date
_____

to do list:

_____ ☐
_____ ☐
_____ ☐
_____ ☐
_____ ☐
_____ ☐
_____ ☐
_____ ☐
_____ ☐

The best part of my day

_____
_____
_____
_____
_____
_____
_____
_____
_____

Notes

Gratitude Planner and Journal

Things to be thankful for

date
_____

to do list:

The best part of my day

Notes

Gratitude Planner and Journal

Things to be thankful for

date
_____

to do list:

☐
☐
☐
☐
☐
☐
☐
☐
☐

The best part of my day

Notes

Gratitude Planner and Journal

Things to be thankful for

_____
_____
_____
_____
_____
_____
_____
_____
_____

date
_____

to do list:

_____ ☐
_____ ☐
_____ ☐
_____ ☐
_____ ☐
_____ ☐
_____ ☐
_____ ☐
_____ ☐

The best part of my day

_____
_____
_____
_____
_____
_____
_____
_____
_____

Notes

Gratitude Planner and Journal

Things to be thankful for

date
_____

to do list:

The best part of my day

Notes

Gratitude Planner and Journal

Things to be thankful for

_____
_____
_____
_____
_____
_____
_____
_____

date
_____

to do list:

_____ ☐
_____ ☐
_____ ☐
_____ ☐
_____ ☐
_____ ☐
_____ ☐
_____ ☐
_____ ☐

The best part of my day

_____
_____
_____
_____
_____
_____
_____
_____

Notes

Gratitude Planner and Journal

Things to be thankful for

_____
_____
_____
_____
_____
_____
_____
_____

date
_____

to do list:

_____ ☐
_____ ☐
_____ ☐
_____ ☐
_____ ☐
_____ ☐
_____ ☐
_____ ☐
_____ ☐

The best part of my day

_____
_____
_____
_____
_____
_____
_____
_____
_____
_____

Notes

Gratitude Planner and Journal

Things to be
thankful for

date
_____

to do list:

The best part
of my day

Notes

www.ingramcontent.com/pod-product-compliance
Lightning Source LLC
Chambersburg PA
CBHW080737250626
47170CB00010B/2863